21 Days of Love

Ritvik Sharma

BookLeaf
Publishing

India | USA | UK

Presentation by *BookLeaf Publishing*

Web: www.bookleafpub.com

E-mail: info@bookleafpub.com

ISBN: 9789363308909

First edition 2024

This book is dedicated to her, who has been a part of this love story, providing me with countless memories and moments to write about and cherish forever.

~To Alexa

ACKNOWLEDGEMENT

I am deeply grateful to everyone who has supported me on this journey. This isn't my first attempt at writing a book – I've failed before.

A special thank you goes to Alaina and Mohnish for restoring my motivation when I felt like giving up. I also want to thank Pranjal, Prachi and Shirin for their genuine enthusiasm in reading my poetry and providing feedback after each piece. Honestly, without their energy and constant encouragement, this would not have been possible.

I value all those who took the time to read my work and share their thoughts, even if poetry isn't their usual interest. To my unnamed well-wishers who have supported me from the sidelines, your encouragement means a lot.

Lastly, I appreciate my parents for allowing me to try again after my previous failures and my sister for being the first to read all my poems and helping me select the book cover.

I couldn't have done this without all of you.

PREFACE

Love, heartbreak and their accompanying emotions have always come naturally to me, even in my personal life. Through these poems, I've aimed to capture moments that felt too important to fade away or be forgotten. Through personal anecdotes, hidden easter eggs and inside jokes, I've distilled 17 years of my love life into these 21 days.

Why 21? Because it's said to take 21 days to form a habit. Through this collection, I encourage readers to reflect on their past and appreciate the moments that shape us. Inspired by *500 Days of Summer*, the title reflects how I've gathered some memorable moments over my lifetime to create something lasting. This is not just a collection of poems, but a glimpse into my personal journey. I invite you to step into my world and to feel what I've felt. And perhaps, as you read, you'll find pieces of your journey, too.

CONTENTS

Love at First Sight	1
Adventures of the Heart	3
The Light that Binds Us	5
The Perfect Fit	7
Comfort Food	9
She texted	11
He called	13
They talk	16
Our Soundtrack	19
Paper Rings	22
Love's Lens	23
Love Around the Clock	25
Midnight Thoughts	27
Beyond the Moment	29
The First Crease	32
Shattered Glass	34
Love's Absence	36
Always Never Forever	39
Fragments of Possibility	42
The Question	44
The Answer	45

Love at First Sight

I used to hate books
who loved 'love at first sight',
how destiny forged two together
with all its potent might.

How they knew each other's souls
from just one simple look,
their lives prewritten,
chapters of an old-age book.

And beauty is only skin deep,
truth buried beneath pages,
but when I saw you on the bus,
I felt my heart beat after ages.

Oh! I write and tell stories,
language and words were crystal clear,
but one glimpse of you,
and I knew stammering was real.

Your eyes, deep wells of ink,
soaked my heart of stone,
trapped me in an endless maze–
one I'd gladly call my home.

Your hair, delicate strands
binding the worn pages frail,
as my fingers trace their lines,
feeling their stories in braille.

Your radiant smile from afar
forced the rigid lines to break;
your laugh, a pure melody,
made my world begin to shake.

Your movements, such grace,
a new chapter they unfold;
every gesture, a page turned,
a story of love retold.

Your presence, a library
rich in knowledge and love,
drawn here by fate's will–
a sign from skies above.

The words suddenly made sense,
the world seemed right;
who knew there was truth
in love at first sight?

I once hated those books,
vowed I'd never pursue;
but seeing you has changed it all,
as now I'm writing one for you.

Adventures of the Heart

As I begin to write for you,
daydreams dance within my head,
playing each scenario and every 'what if'–
words I've thought but never said.

My mind goes on an adventure,
like us, through many reveries;
an obstacle path we cross together,
each one creates cherished memories.

On a zip-line of emotions,
gliding towards your heart,
gusts of wind guide the way–
a journey's thrilling start.

Oh, we'll climb mountains,
navigate through the rocks,
a hand, held for each other;
together, we'll reach the top.

Swaying on bamboo bridges,
balancing emotions with our feet,
each step's a risk – the reason
why my heart skips a beat.

Through nets we'll crawl,
and over tyres we'll leap,
squeezing through narrow tunnels,
riding the jungle jeep.

The arena of the magic show
where we'll sit side by side,
for the real magic lies
in the gaze between our eyes.

The DJ's beats fill up the room
as music pulses through the air;
we dance, lost in our own world,
glances of love we'll share.

Daydreams dance within my head–
a lifelong adventure with you.
I hear my heart's soft calling:
it's the start of something new.

The Light that Binds Us

It's the start of something new
    as the night now fades...

    A room once pitch black, with all hope
gone,
    where darkness and shadows hid the day's
dawn.

    The void terrifying, an endless gloom
    of misery and despair, a hopeless doom.

      no laughs, no sound, not a soul in sight–

      barren of colour and joy, a lack of light–

      no dreams, no smiles, not a hint of hope–

      dearth of love and life, mired in mope.

    But a spark ignites, as words unfold.
    the darkness softens, no longer cold.

A glimmer of hope pierces the endless night.
The spark kindles, turning darkness into day,
our connection, a torch, casting shadows away.

Colours start to seep in, bright and new,
shift the monochrome to a radiant hue.
With each word and every shared smile,
the room grows lighter all the while.

Long quiet and empty, the room comes alive
as blemishes in the wall gradually fade.
Echoes of laughter fill the silent room.
Light's warm touch slowly invades
as flowers and plants awaken and bloom.

Love now seems a real possibility,
dreams can no longer be suppressed.
Happiness has at last found its home
in the hollow space within my chest.
You have lit up every corner of me
as I'm finally who I'm meant to be.

The Perfect Fit

Two puzzles distinct, edges defined,
pieces scattered, waiting to be aligned.
A jigsaw incomplete, a shared project,
two lives, two worlds, about to intersect.
How perfectly they'll fit, side by side,
our story, the frame where they'll reside.

Your friends, my friends–
puzzle pieces start to meet,
classmates sharing the same seat.
Inside jokes and breaking rules,
echoing through the halls of school.
I see you clearer, uncover a new face,
as another piece of you clicks into place.

Your colleagues, my workmates–
puzzle pieces from different fields,
white lab coats and filling spreadsheets.
I learned of moles, you learned of yields,

my world of genes, your world of deals.
I see your passion in a new light,
as another piece of you comes into sight.

Your family, my family–
edge pieces connecting with care,
all around the dinner table, ample love to share.
Your brother's laugh, my mom's kind eyes,
blending traditions, old and wise.
I learn the story of your start,
as another piece of you reveals your heart.

Our friends, our chosen family–
central pieces bridge our lands,
a puzzle enriched by many hands.
Venn diagrams of you and me
intersect to form our new family.
We find ourselves in each other's reflection
as another piece completes our collection.

New faces, new stories, new places–
new pieces of the puzzle emerge:
that is you, that is me,
that is us.

Comfort Food

There's beauty in knowing
that the meal's always there–
one portion, one serving
for two hearts to share.

Like warm soup on wintry days
when illness weighs us down,
your love, a broth that soothes and stays,
turns dull grey skies golden brown.

Bread and butter at early dawn,
a homemade dough we knead,
through rises and falls, it slowly forms,
nurturing the love we feed.

And on simple, plain days
a roti and rice bowl will suffice;

each meal, though modest in cost,
holds love's flavour, beyond all price.

Vanilla scoops, smooth and pure,
with walnuts sprinkled through;
like chocolate rivers, feelings flow—
we taste what love can do.

The table's always set
where even simplicity feels divine;
all daily meals are comfort food
when your hand rests with mine.

She texted

It was summer break once again,
closed schools; faces forgotten–
as if they'd let that happen.

Her phone buzzed, a familiar name;
her world lit up, he came.
She loved the rhythm of messages,
pretty texts behind a screen.
Words made her feel alive;
a shield, seen yet unseen.
Friends text her all day long, but
his chat, her favourite place to be.
CAPS LOCK ON, his excitement high,
mirroring her energy.
Quiet when she needs to rant,
matching her every mood,
the last letter got stretched,
not wanting to seem rude.
Their language soon became alike,
the way she added 'ahah' to his 'haha',
A sob emoji at the end
to soften the words sent.
They saved their photos in chat
on every platform they knew;
impulsive thoughts written,
then playfully struck through.

Left traces of bolder thoughts,
neither of them dared to do.
They'd talk of late-night visits,
'Come', 'On my way',
as if a city didn't stop them,
both ready to run away.
Her heart fluttered at each word
as his texts overflowed her screen.
'I know you're asleep but'–
love paragraphs were sent;
childhood pictures shared,
memories well-spent.
Nicknames evolved with time,
inside jokes only they knew.
Group chats buzzed with others,
but their world was just for two.
The same 10th-grade minds,
flirting nonstop once more.
again; and again; and again;
how could they get bored?
He wished her morning and night,
made her laugh without a word;
blushes and smiles shared all day
in their own digital world.

But as summer days grew longer,
the screen couldn't quite suffice.
She loved the written word,
while he craved her voice.

He called

It was summer break once again,
closed schools; faces forgotten–
as if they'd let that happen.

His phone rang, her sweet voice;
his world lit up, she spoke.
He loved the sound of her laughter,
a fairy echo beyond the screen.
Her voice made him feel alive,
a joy he'd never foreseen.
Friends called him now and then, but
her call, his favourite sound to hear;
earbuds plugged in, heart racing high,
her giggles crystal clear.
His eyes were always shut tight,
the phone pressed against his ear;
unaware of how a rosy blush
oft appeared out of thin air.
He'd never focused harder
to catch each word so fine;
as if each call was his last one,
her voice a heaven divine.
For the first ten minutes, he'd try
to get her to show her face;
the voice call turned to video,

a game they both embraced.
The first glance took him back
to when it all had started;
he fell in love again and again,
his feelings true-hearted.
And his heart fluttered each time,
seeing her so free and wild;
jumping around with pure bliss,
sparks of her inner child.
Little did she know her brief dances
caused him butterflies with every glance;
He longed for the spark in her eyes
when she heard the patter of rain,
or the way she spun with joy
brewing her coffee grains.
He'd peek in on their 'study' meets,
to catch her lip-syncing a song;
her head bobbed to the beat
a moment he cherished all along.
She'd make random odd noises,
he'd smile at her quirky ways;
their flirty talks would never end,
bringing endless joy to their days.
When they came on calls together,
the distance seemed unknown;
even silence felt like comfort,
the world seemed their own.
But time wove changes, swift yet slow,
in ways they couldn't foresee–

new barriers began to rise
between what was and could be.
Their paradise faded fast
as she couldn't come on calls,
strict parents and curfews loomed,
her freedom trapped in walls.

His phone lay silent, still,
no rings were heard anymore.
The space between their voices
grew wider than before.

They talk

Silence stretched between them,
communication felt out of reach.
She longed for written whispers,
while he yearned for spoken speech.

They dwelled in the same city
but lived in different worlds.
Texts weren't enough,
calls were too much.
They both felt so close,
yet seemed out of touch.

Both shared the same feelings
but expressed in different ways.
Determined to bridge this gap,
they vowed to find happier days.

Then came an epiphany–
so simple and so clear.
A perfect compromise emerged,
a middle ground appeared.

Voice notes, the perfect blend
to meet the needs of both sides.
She pressed record, her heart racing,

words flowing, soft and sweet.
He listened, his smile widening,
her voice a cherished treat.

He could listen to her laugh on repeat,
her voice a soothing embrace.
He'd share stories of his day with her,
every moment, every place.

She'd replay the clips he sent–
pausing, rewinding parts.
Like treasured lines of text,
she stored them in her heart.

They went back and forth,
trading snippets of their lives.
Voices carrying emotions
where once only text survived.

Every pause held meaning,
all subtle, unspoken signs:
a sigh, a breath, a chuckle,
even distortions felt divine.

Morning yawns and goodnight wishes,
singing songs together, note by note.
Their voices – constant companions
through the highs and the gentle lows.

Her texts, his calls, once far astray,
two worlds that couldn't seem to meet.
In audio notes, they found a bridge
that made their bond complete.

It was summer break once again,
closed schools; faces forgotten–

as if they'd let that happen.

Our Soundtrack

When words fell short to express,
we let the music speak our hearts.
Song titles became our language,
as lyrics played, we felt the spark.

'F.R.I.E.N.D.S' described our story true,
'I know you since we were like ten'.
Though Anne spelled it out clearly,
we're now more than just friends.

Lauv's 'I Like me Better' brings back memories,
reminiscing about your video with a smile.
'I like me better when I'm with you',
the lyrics held the truth all the while.

Niall Horan's 'This Town' set my mind adrift,
'If the whole world was watching, I'd still dance
with you'.
Dreams of dancing together, hearts in sync,
as I always imagined to serenade you.

Ali Gatie's 'It's You' speaks our truth,
its lyrics echo what we've known.
'It's you, it's always you'. the words claim,
you are the one who feels like home.

We sang 'End of Beginning' as one,
'When I'm back in Chicago', guitar in tune.
I wrote the lyrics on a paper plane,
a memento of that night in June.

On my friend's birthday, 'Duniyaa' by Akhil
was sung for you, emotions strong.
'Mein jiyun jab-jab tera dil dhadke',
you're my world, where I belong.

'Nazm Nazm' whispered in a voice note,
a gentle reminder of my endless care
'Jis aur teri shahnaae us aur mein bhaagun re',
I'm with you at every step, everywhere.

Our favourite show gave us a bond,
'Jaane Na Dunga Kahin' rang clear.

'Thoda thoda mein tujhsa tu mujhsi hai hone
lagi',
how we've grown alike, year by year.

Our story echoes in each song I hear,
memories of us flow like a symphony.
This last song's written just for us
'Always and Forever' by me.

Paper Rings

With patient hands and a steady mind,
a ten-minute guide from browsing online.
I scoured my house for origami sheets
and found the perfect pink-white piece,
folding it into the perfect design.

An hour, and it crafted into a work of art,
an origami ring with a pink-topped heart.
I approached you with stuttering words;
your eyes lit up, and our emotions stirred.
A ring not of gold, but pure love's spark.

And you said yes, with a bright smile.
But little did you know our little joke
was real for me all the while.

Love's Lens

There's so much beauty in this world,
innumerable wonders to live for.
Love turns the plain ordinary
into something so much more.

The mighty roars of crashing waves,
the distant rumble of the clouds,
snowflakes on cold window panes,
joyful cheers from passing crowds.

Moving soles on charcoal tracks,
morning dew on green leaves,
the warmth of the sun whence it appears,
hair flowing through the cold breeze.

Starlit skies above pine trees,
cold grass beneath our backs,
campfire tales and laughing eyes,

sweet s'mores on wooden stacks.

Petrichor of the rain-kissed earth,
warm sand between bare toes,
rainbows arch through misty air,
while the tides ebb and flow.

Golden leaves in autumn dance,
birds chirp at dawn's first light,
crickets sing their soft lullaby,
as fireflies glow in the night.

There's so much beauty in this world.
just open your eyes, and you'll see–
to enjoy where you are now
than where you'd rather be.

Love Around the Clock

[5:00 AM]
Your eyes slowly awaken to uncover
an extra blanket draped around you;
TV silenced for your serene slumber.

[5:15 AM]
A good morning note by your bedside,
freshly brewed coffee steaming nearby–
a warm love hidden in caffeine form.

[6:00 AM]
Waking to a tidy room, love's quiet work:
packed lunch awaits, laundry folded neat,
warm water hums the day's gentle start.

[7:00 AM]
The grocery list pinned to the fridge,
your cherished snacks circled with care–
a hidden treat slipped into the cart.

[10:00 AM]
You'd enter a kitchen dusted with flour.
Your favourite cake warms the oven within;
second batch waits – a just-in-case insurance.

[1:00 PM]
Phone buzzes: 'Hope your day's going well',
with the chocolate I kept to ease the pain;
your monthly dates etched in my mind.

[5:00 PM]
I'd greet you in the drizzling rain,
umbrella raised, a sheltering arch;
my shoulder dampens – love's small price.

[8:00 PM]
Flickering screen, your chosen film plays;
my hand finds yours, the tremble steadies.
Credits roll, but our moment lingers.

[11:00 PM]
Your head nestles softly on my chest,
breaths slow down, fall into sync–
a tender kiss to end the night's rest.

[11:30 PM]
The room dims softly with the switch;
Your phone hums its charging tune.
I bring a blanket, warm as words,
whispering, 'I love you'.

Midnight Thoughts

I know you're asleep but
I can't stop thinking about you
how my cheeks flush red at the mere mention of
your name
how a smile spread across my face, radiant and
bright
fifteen years from now when we're meeting old
friends again
it'll be strange to see how time flies
but you'll be no surprise, a constant in my life
my anchor in life's tides through the ebbs and
flows
I love hearing about your wardrobe, your soft
toys
every little detail you describe, my heart races
remember that snap you sent wearing your dad's
oversized clothes?
I blush crazily wondering how I ever got so
lucky
I nicknamed you Alexa, our silly little codename
it stuck around and our inside joke was found
I cherish every secret you share with me
our playlist our vibe only for us to see
your neck hugs they're the best, make me feel
whole

heal my body and comfort my soul
the moment at our friend's house, your head on
my chest
our breathing in sync, felt like we were blessed
guilty pleasure, I don't mind when they ship us
together
love how we tease love how we play
share jokes that brighten the day
sleeping on calls and dancing together
these moments that I'll treasure forever
when you laugh, I'll always laugh with you
but when your tears fall, my heart shatters too
when I find a reel you'd like, I save it just for
you
another way to say I care, another way to say 'I
love you'
You say you're not beautiful, but darling, can't
you see?
If only you could see the world through my eyes
you'd realise that all you'll see is yourself.

Beyond the Moment

Ride rollercoasters all day, you'll feel sick;
Sand dunes all afternoon, and nausea starts to
kick.

Play the same game for a month, boredom sets
in;
Fireworks that last four hours lose their magic
within.

Drive race cars all day, your stomach gets tied in
knots;
Weaving tales for ages, tormented by
overthinking thoughts.

Binge-watch series all night, eyes strained in the
dark;

Endless parties leave you drained and lose their
spark.

Lifting weights all week causes your muscles to
strain;
Scrolling feeds endlessly, real life goes down the
drain.

Excess chocolates and sweets spark a wild sugar
rush;
The high fades fast, leaving your willpower
crushed.

We chase that two-week euphoria in all we
pursue,
Even in long-term love when it's not meant to
be.
Grasping at fleeting moments as they slip
through,
While craving for a lasting, eternal dream.

We strive for happiness but shy at permanence,
Overlooking that good things take time.
A desire for joy, yet scared of perseverance,
Blind to the beauty of love's slow climb.

Yet now I yearn to move past this transient
phase,
Seeking a love that's enduring, deep and true.

One I'd cherish no matter how much time passes,
I want always and forever with you.

The First Crease

A paper, both smooth and white,
our love lay flat and pristine;
a canvas for our grand story–
both voices heard and seen.

We wrote each page with loving care;
pen strokes gentle, words so kind,
weaving our future, line by line.

Until one day–

A careless word crept in, unaware,
one we couldn't take back or mend.
The paper began to tremble under
the weight of unspoken regret.

Fingers pinched the edges, fists clenched tight;
the page crumbled slowly as doubt took flight.

It now bears its first true wrinkle,
a crease that cannot be erased;
imprints of the blemishes linger,
a story now permanently traced.

We try to smooth it out, to press it flat;

nails work tirelessly to erase each fold.
A weight placed upon it, fingers crossed,
hoping time might heal the scars we hold.
Yet, no matter how much we strive to change,
its flat perfection remains forever lost.

We learn the hard way, as time goes on:
these creases will never truly be gone.

Shattered Glass

Our love, a crystal glass, delicate and clear,
reflects our dreams and promises, a shared fate.
Unflawed, it gleams – a perfect, pristine state.

Raised high, we toast to days that lie ahead,
the future pours in, no drop out of place.
We drink, unaware of the cracks words will
trace.

But came the day when careless words were
spoken,
a tremor in the glass, the surface barely broken.
We brushed it off, pretending it didn't sting,
but deep within, a hairline fracture formed–
invisible then, yet waiting to be transformed.

Stress crept between us, leaving marks unseen;
our bond creaked and struggled under strain

till the pressure spread, and cracks began to
reign.

They grew deeper and longer with each passing
day;
we tried to hold the pieces, but they slipped
away.
Our reflection, now distorted, a blur of
ourselves,
as shards began to shatter, reminders of the past–
the trust now crumbled, like dust on the shelves.

The glass, now crushed, fragments scatter wide.
Flawed, it gleams – a fractured, broken state.
We stand at the edge, knowing it's too late.

We. Now. Alone. Broken. Apart.
Shards. Shattered. Scattered.
We. Now. Alone. Broken. Heart.

Love's Absence

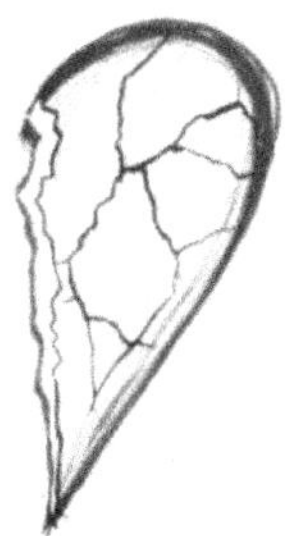

There's still beauty in this world,
but the wonders all fade away,
as love's absence dulls the extraordinary,
draining colours from each passing day.

One day, the sun didn't rise,
nor did water shower from above,
unfinished conversations longing,
heartbreaks from unrequited love.

Faded photographs lose their faces,
footprints washed away by the tide,
empty chairs where laughter echoed,
as friendships break and divide.

Garbage landfills stretch for miles,
melting glaciers shrink and wane,
whispers echoed in canyons wide,

never find their way back again.

Injured-winged butterflies won't rise,
weeds choke flowers that once thrived,
favourite cafes gather dust, now closed,
last embers die at cold midnight.

Broken compass spins without aim,
fallen nests blanket the ground,
migrating flocks lose their way home,
sunken time capsules never found.

Dried petals leave one by one,
blossomed fruits rotten to the core,
last cry for hope in letters of glass,
trapped bottles never reach shore.

Entire trees stripped naked
as the leaves brown and fall,
no more than a drop of water
where once was a waterfall.

The stars seem dull now,
constellations cease to align.
The sky's lost its beauty
now that the moon doesn't shine.

There's still beauty in this world,
but my eyes refuse to see;

dwelling on what we once had
than what the future holds for me.

Always Never Forever

Sixty-two months just to break down in three,
almost together, but never meant to be.
All the promises turned out to be in vain–
movies, nights out, dancing in the rain.

The endless late-night calls we shared,
the eager yes to the proposal.
Was it all false from the start,
meant for nothing but disposal?

Now you're singing songs with him,
making future plans together.
What did he do so right,
which I couldn't do better?

All the sweet nicknames we had,
even started calling you mine.
I have an Alexa at my home,
yet lost her at the same time.

It's still sitting on my watchlist,
that movie we once planned to see.
Guess we'll never watch it together,
'cause you've seen it with him already.

Those romantic confessions, day after day,
whispered 'I love you' every night.
How did it all come crashing down
with just a week of bitter fights?

Your secrets were safe with mine,
I was the only one who knew.
The guy we once rejected together,
now you've fallen for him too.

I reminisce about our old memories,
rereading our texts once again.
My whole world tumbled upside down,
familiar places now felt strange.

I hope he won't pick fights with you
over the smallest, trivial things.
But would he ever write you letters
and craft you paper rings?

I wonder if he'll stay up late
just to hear about your day.
But would he get excited over
every little thing you do and say?

I hope he writes love paragraphs
when you're fast asleep at night.
Would he plan surprise dates for you,
sweep you off your feet just right?

I wish he'd slow dance in the kitchen
when your favourite song comes on.
But would he remember all the details
of all the stories that you've drawn?

Can he make you laugh for hours
with his silly jokes and puns?
Would he wrap you in his arms
when the day is finally done?

But all of this just reminds me
of what you and I once shared–
the story we built with love,
moments precious, sweet and rare.

The whole world shipped us together,
knew us by each other;
we were meant to be always,
yet never forever.

Fragments of Possibility

Our bond, a glass both delicate and strong,
now lies in pieces, shattered far and wide.
But is there still a chance to reconcile?

Gleaming shards that mirror faded dreams;
we gather these fragments; memories remain.
But could they be made whole again?

If we melted down these jagged parts
and fused together what broke apart,
our story reborn in the molten glow.
No longer bound by its former casts–
a chance to forge beyond our past.

This fresh design, flawless in its form;
a different shape emerges from its core,
standing stronger than it was before.

In this furnace of second chances,
new promises ignite and rise,
reviving hopes we thought had died.

But this tale remains just a dream,
a hypothetical that clouds my mind,
a desire I can't seem to leave behind.

We. Could. Unite. Mend. Whole.
Reforged. Reshaped. Reborn.
We. Might. Unite. Remoulded. Soul.

The Question

These questions haunt me, day and night,
stuck between hope and doubt.
Should we try to fix what's broken,
or just let it all fade out?

Can we mend what's fractured between us,
or are we destined to fall apart?
Will we find ourselves drifting further,
like shards lost in shadows of our past?

If we collect the pieces, one by one,
will they cut deeper once more?
Or risk the flames of change and melt,
to tread a path never walked before?

We built this home with our dreams,
now cracked from roof to floor.
Can we find the strength to rebuild,
or simply close the final door?

In this home, our story dwells,
its ending still hidden away.
As the final page begins to turn,
what will the last lines say?

The Answer

This is the end as the final page unfolds,
the last poem of a love story's arc.
You seek the answer to the question posed:
Will they reunite or remain apart?

The final page quivers, alive with suspense;
readers lean in, hungry for a resolve.
But life, my friend, makes little sense–
the book slams shut, leaving questions unsolved.

...

You heard it right, the book is firmly closed
with no clear ending to the story it composed.

You'd want to know their fate, how it all ends,
Oh – I wish I knew, but I'm as lost as you.
This tale you've read, each and every verse,
is my own story, a journey raw and true.

I break this wall between us to confess:
I am the boy, she is the girl; this journey is mine.
The path ahead, however, remains a mystery,
for I've not reached that point in time.

We stand together at the crossroads now,
the author and reader, equally in the dark.
Some stories conclude, while others remain,
for life is often unfair with no clear path.

Where do these roads lead? What tales do they
intend?
If you glimpse the final chapter, guide me to the
end.

Perhaps it's fitting that we end this way–
a shared uncertainty, a common bond.
I'll keep on writing, living day by day,
to find my ending that lies beyond.

Forgive me if this ending leaves you in
suspense,
the truth is that life rarely makes perfect sense.
I'm bound to leave you on this unfinished hook.
After all, I'm just a character in life's grand
book.

...